Supported by Arriva, London Transport Museum and Time Out London.

Designed by Magpie Studio, London.
Printed and bound in China.

www.routemasters.co.uk

ISBN: 978-1-85983-610-1

LAST STOP
RALF OBERGFELL

London is a city with many ghosts. On 9 December 2005, the Routemaster bus became another phantom of Oxford Street. After close to fifty years, it was famous the world over, its image and name as synonymous with the capital as Big Ben, Trafalgar Square, pigeons and exorbitant house prices. In many respects, these roll-top baths in guardsmen's red had been living on borrowed time since the day the last one filed off the production line in 1968. Their executions were stayed so often that it came to seem as if they could live forever. But now they have officially joined the ranks of the undead. The handful that linger haunt the city, as if tethered by chains, on two heritage routes.

Unlike most spectres, however, these blood-red tykes are gone by dusk. And, like black cabs, not seen south of the river. But in London and beyond, the Routemaster is still a powerful talisman. Just a few months after its official retirement, the Routemaster was voted an Icon of England and competed against Concorde and the Chopper bicycle in something called the Great British Design Quest.

And to evoke its name is to call up powerful notions of classic style, indigenous engineering ingenuity, civic pride and the thrill of a hop-on, hop-off ride, the open platform a potent symbol of the liberties of the city itself.

Illustrating their currency, Boris Johnson, equipped as he is with the hair (and name) of a mad scientist in a James Whale film, launched his London mayoral campaign in 2007 promising to bring the Routemaster back to life again. The Son of the Routemaster was back on the slab, in the political lab, at least.

Just how or why something as mundane as a bus came to occupy such an exalted position in London's emotional and socio-cultural firmament isn't entirely easy to explain. Well, certainly not straightforward, anyway. One thing I'd like to suggest is that looking good in colour film didn't do it any harm. But before we get on to all of that, it's probably best if we start with the nuts and bolts.

The Routemaster was the last bus to be built for London by Londoners in London. It was the last bus to be staffed by both a driver and a conductor. And it was the last bus to go into service with the engine and half-cab for the driver at the front and an open platform for passengers to enter and exit at the rear. It really represented the culmination of a line of similar vehicles made specifically for London dating back to 1910, when the London General Omnibus Company produced their rather dull-sounding B-type bus. As the final bus to be staffed by a conductor, its lineage can even be traced to Shillibeer's first horse omnibus from 1829. But, most significantly, it was the last bus to be wholly conceived for the capital – Savile Row-tailored, if you like – by the once monolithic London Transport.

All public transport in London had come under the unified control of the London Passenger Transport Board in 1933. The largest transport organisation on the planet and a public corporation along the lines of the BBC, London Transport was able to use Treasury funds to create a fully integrated network that was, for a time, without equal anywhere in the world. London Transport's guiding light, its conscience and its superego, even after his death in 1941, was its chief executive Frank Pick.

Pick was a severe, cold and slightly intimidating man. Raised among devout Congregational Methodists, he was a dedicated administrator who possessed a visionary eye and zeal for good modern design. Believing that ordinary Londoners deserved the best and that their lives could be enriched by surrounding them with simple, beautiful and well-made objects, Pick insisted on uniform levels of coherence and excellence across the board. The roundel of the Underground logo, the distinct Johnston typeface of its signage, Harry Beck's diagrammatical tube map and Charles Holden's incomparable stations for the Piccadilly line were all commissioned under Pick's watch. In 1942, the architectural historian Nikolaus Pevsner dubbed him 'the Lorenzo the Magnificent of our age'. And the standards and the culture that he established at London Transport were central to the design of the Routemaster.

In the 1930s, the efforts of London Transport's Bus and Coach Division, headed by the equally formidable and no less exacting Albert Arthur Durrant, had culminated in the creation of a flagship bus, the RT, in 1939. For many, the RT, in its post-war incarnations, is the London bus. Nearly twice as many were built as its usurper the Routemaster and it tarried in the capital for forty years. It is also the London Bus on which Cliff, Una and gang rode Europe-wards for some sun in *Summer Holiday* (just to get that out of the way now).

During the Second World War, the corporation's bus works at Chiswick were turned over to aircraft production and helped to build Handley Page Halifax bombers. Through this work, LT engineers and designers came into contact with the latest innovations in aircraft manufacturing, including the use of lightweight aluminium and component construction. These ideas were soon put to good use on Civvy Street when bus building recommenced after the war.

In 1947, and in the spirit of a period when bold forward-thinking initiatives like the NHS were coming into fruition, the very first memos about the need for a brand new alloy bus for London began circulating at London Transport. It would take four years of research work and countless discussions with manufacturers and men from ministries before a final course for the Routemaster was steered, another three after that before a prototype was finished, and then another four before the bus entered production. It took less time to get Sputnik into space. But the final bus would be a capacious, fuel-efficient, highly-advanced, chassis-less construction. Tooled in lightweight aluminum, it was comprised, rather like a

Meccano set, of completely interchangeable parts. Such ingenious engineering was partly why the Routemaster, originally designed for just seventeen years' service, lasted so long. Like the planks of the Ship of Theseus, they could be refurbished piece by piece over time without disturbing the integrity of the whole.

Having already re-activated pre-war plans to scrap the remaining trams (the last ran on 5 July 1952), LT decided to do away with the city's electric trolleybuses as well. Pollution-free and practically silent, the trolleybuses were a safe and environmentally sound means of transport. In retrospect, this was a dreadful mistake. But at a point when car ownership was rising in the capital – parking restrictions (yellow lines) had already been introduced on some central roads by 1947 – the wire-borne trolleys were thought an obstruction to traffic.

Acutely aware that it was facing increasing competition from motorists, London Transport went out of its way to ensure that its new bus (now to replace the trolleys too) matched and even surpassed levels of comfort found in your average Austin or Morris. The more luxurious the buses, the reasoning went, the greater chance they stood of luring people from their cars. To that end, the Routemaster was fitted with a heating system – a rarity on all but the top of the range motors then. Independent suspension and a fully automatic gearbox were installed to provide a smoother ride and make the bus easier to drive. And, for safety, power hydraulic brakes that virtually eliminated failure in icy conditions, previously developed for aircraft, were fitted as standard.

A prevailing stipulation at London Transport was that the bus must be an attractive piece of street furniture (a phrase, incidentally, favoured by Frank Pick), and one of the few industrial design consultants, Douglas Scott, was engaged to style the Routemaster for them.

From his Potterton Boiler to his GPO call box and his Rediffusion radio sets, Scott's product designs are models of practical, restrained style. In the 1930s, Scott had been employed in the London office of Raymond Loewy, the great American pioneer of 'streamlining' and the man who supplied Lucky Strike cigarettes with their logo and Shell Petrol with their, well, shell. And the shapely body that Scott sculpted for the Routemaster attests to a mastery of the undulating curve he acquired during his stint with Loewy.

With the interiors, Scott also excelled himself. The final colour scheme – 'Burgundy lining panels, Chinese Green window surrounds and Sung Yellow ceilings', as the official description rather fancifully had it – was chic, heartening and durable. Meanwhile, the tartan mocquette of dark red and yellow he created for the leather-trimmed seats exuded a debonair Aberdeen Angus air but hid dirt and proved immensely hardwearing.

The prototype Routemaster was officially unveiled at the Commercial Motor Show in Earl's Court on 24 September 1954 under the banner 'London's Bus of the Future'. The name Routemaster was chosen in preference to Roadmaster only a couple of weeks before the show. 'Masters' seem to have been in vogue that season; a Rowe Hillmaster truck was another vehicle at Earl's Court, while cinema-goers that year watched an apartment-bound Jimmy Stewart trim his stubble with a Sunbeam Shavemaster in Alfred Hitchcock's *Rear Window*.

For all of its interchangeable aluminium, some commentators felt the Routemaster was rather old-fashioned looking, a tad trad – which could explain its longevity; free from the more obvious 1950s gimcracks it, perhaps, aged better than its peers.

Sharing its birthday with that other stylish baby boomer, the Stratocaster guitar, the Routemaster's lifespan in effect mirrors the rock 'n' roll years: a total of 2875 were built between 1954 and 1968. Like the new breed of teenagers, it was a child of austerity that came of age in an era defined by unprecedented levels of affluence. The downside of this, for a bus, at least, was that those who could afford to were increasingly choosing to travel under their own steam. The number of cars registered in London doubled between 1945 and 1960. Rising home ownership, suburbanisation and television were also reducing the number of bus journeys taken, with Londoners choosing to spend a greater part of their leisure time at home.

With almost full employment, London Transport also found it difficult to obtain staff for jobs with relatively low rates of pay and often long and antisocial hours. This combination of falling passenger numbers and staff shortages would ultimately prove fatal for the Routemaster. Off-the-shelf one-person-operated vehicles would come to be seen as the panacea to London Transport's ills.

But just a few months after 8 February 1956, when the RM made her maiden voyage on Route 2 from Golders Green to Crystal Palace, London Transport began to recruit employees directly from Barbados. This scheme was extended to Malta, Jamaica and Trinidad in the 1960s. Playing its own part in the repopulating of London, the Routemaster arrived at the moment when the city was becoming a far more polychromatic place.

Returning to London from the Spanish Civil War in 1939, George Orwell had been heartened to find that 'the men in bowler hats, the pigeons in Trafalgar Square, the red buses, the blue policemen' were all still intact. But the colour most people associate with London (and Britain for that matter) after the war and into the 1950s was bomb-dust, austerity grey. When the Zurich-born photographer Robert Frank reached London from Paris in 1951, he was astonished to find it 'black, white and grey.' His own snaps of fog-shrouded London double-deckers and Magritte-like city gents from this period mine the drear beauty of those three shades for all they're worth.

But the arrival of the Clean Air Act in 1956 and Kodacolor film the year afterwards not only transformed how London actually was but also the image that the city now presented of itself. By the 1960s, the black and white of the *Picture Post* and *The Lavender Hill Mob* had been superseded by colour – Technicolor, Kodak Instamatic, *Sunday Times* Colour Section, James Bond movie colour. Although it features the wrong bus, *Summer Holiday* exemplifies the phenomenon. The film pointedly begins in black and white and, *à la The Wizard of Oz*, bursts into colour the instant Cliff Richard arrives on screen, driving a red RT bus.

As London's pendulum began to swing, these red open-platform double-deckers became an essential, unavoidable component in any representation of the city's giddy 'happening' scene in print or on film. The bus seemed to sum up the free-and-easy, catch-me-if-you-can, hop-on, hop-off optimism of those days.

The notion of actually using a London bus to promote the nation can be dated to the Festival of Britain in 1951: four double-deckers toured around Europe in the months leading up the festival. But in the 1960s, the Routemaster acted as a kind of perpetual diesel-powered Beefeater for Blighty across the globe. In November 1962, one of the first major exhibitions of British Pop Art in America opened at the San Francisco Museum of Modern Art. 'British Art Today',

including work by Patrick Heron and Patrick Wall, was trailed by 'London Week'; a trade/cultural jamboree replete with a Routemaster shipped over for the event. Internationally and locally, then, the Routemaster became the ace face at a time when London was becoming the place to be. Quintessentially, classically British and yet modern, it was *The Avengers* on wheels.

Still, by 1971, while John Lennon was breezily telling *Rolling Stone* that the dream was over and 'Chirpy Chirpy, Cheep Cheep' was storming up the charts, London Transport was confidently predicting that they'd all be gone before 1978. Somehow, in 1981 most of them were still about. By the 1990s, only 600 or so lingered in the capital. But, in the words of Tennyson, 'boldly they rode and well' and life in London without them seemed almost as unthinkable as evicting the ravens from the Tower. In the 2002 horror film *28 Days Later*, an overturned and abandoned Routemaster provided the most potent symbol of London's ravaging by zombies. *Time Out* magazine put Duke Baysee, the harmonica-playing conductor of the 38 bus, at number 66 in their Top 100 Reasons to Live in the Capital.

In 2002, however, Transport for London announced that the Routemasters, failing to meet European legislation on disabled access, would be phased out. Before the last Routemaster made its final journey, on 9 December 2005, from Marble Arch to Streatham, questions had been asked in the House of Commons. The *Evening Standard* had a campaign devoted to their preservation. Ten thousand people had signed a petition against their scrapping. Cliff Richard had vowed never to record again. And the majority of the photographs that fill this book had been taken.

I first met Ralf while I was out chasing after those ever-diminishing shadows, as Routemaster route after Routemaster route was gradually spirited away. We were both convinced something quite unique was being lost, and were trying to document that in our own different ways. And for my part, I still remain rather envious of how his photographs capture something that (naturally) evades prose. Or my prose, anyway. For you can write all you like about the design, the engineering, Frank Pick, Douglas Scott, Cliff Richard, and how it fits into London's story – all of which is important and relevant – but the Routemaster earned its place in most Londoners' hearts by simply doing its job. And it's those daily interactions, the attrition of little experiences, the everyday glimpses on the streets, the chances to hop aboard, the scrambles for the top deck, the nods to the conductor, that Ralf's photographs nail so well. The Routemaster in London has, of course, long since come to its last stop. The heritage routes, thankfully, provide the opportunity to experience them in their natural habitat but not as essential components of the living and breathing city. What was once everyday is now extraordinary, and we need photographs like these to remind us of that. Far spookier for its proximity, the day before is still yesterday, and that is history. And long after the memories have faded, these images will continue to bring the ghosts of the past back to life again.

Last Stops: The Routemaster's Final Journeys

Number 159
Marble Arch – Streatham Station, 9 December 2005.

Number 38
Victoria Station – Clapton Pond, 28 October 2005.

Number 13
Golders Green Station – Aldwych, 21 October 2005.

Number 14
Putney Heath – Tottenham Court Road Station, 22 July 2005.

Number 22
Putney Common – Piccadilly Circus, 2 July 2005.

Number 19
Finsbury Park Station – Battersea Bridge, 1 April 2005.

Number 36
Queen's Park Station – New Cross, 28 January 2005.

Number 12
Notting Hill Gate – Dulwich Plough, 5 November 2004.

Number 9
Hammersmith Bus Station – Aldwych, 3 September 2004.

Number 73
Victoria Station – Stoke Newington Common, 3 September 2004.

Number 390
Marble Arch – Archway, 3 September 2004.

Number 137
Streatham Hill – Oxford Circus, 9 July 2004.

Number 7
Russell Square – East Acton Station, 2 July 2004.

Number 8
Bow Church – Victoria, 4 June 2004.

Number 6
Aldwych – Kensal Rise, 22 March 2004.

Number 98
Willesden – Holborn Red Lion Square, 22 March 2004.

Number 94
Acton Green – Trafalgar Square, 23 January 2004.

Number 23
Liverpool Street Station – Westbourne Park, 2 November 2003.

Number 11
Liverpool Street Station – Fulham Broadway, 31 October 2003.

Number 15
Paddington Station – East Ham, 29 August 2003.

Since 15 November 2005 Heritage Routemasters have been running on Route 15: Trafalgar Square – Tower Hill and Route 9: Royal Albert Hall – Aldwych.

Travis Elborough is the author of
*The Bus We Loved: London's Affair
with the Routemaster* (Granta 2005).
He is a freelance journalist and writes
for *The Guardian*, *New Statesman*,
Sunday Times, *Zembla* and *The Oldie*.

Right
Wing 01

Left
Wing 02

Introduction
Ben Walters

There are three items of street furniture, created during the last century of the British Empire, whose designs continue to define the global idea of a London street. In 1853, the pillar box – invented by the novelist and long-serving Post Office employee Anthony Trollope – was introduced to allow letters to be mailed without the need for a trip to a Post Office branch. In 1936, the K6 telephone box designed by Sir Giles Gilbert Scott marked the end of 15 years of experimentation to find the ideal vehicle for public telephony. And 20 years after that, in 1956, the Routemaster bus began service on the streets of the capital.

Coloured an unmissably proud yet regally dignified red, distinguished by curved, weighty contours and, most importantly, eminently fit for their purposes, these three design icons complemented each other with remarkable harmony. All three were soon inspiring a level of affection unusual for such ostensibly utilitarian, everyday objects, but none so much as the Routemaster. The RM was far from London's first double-decker, but – as Travis Elborough has so eloquently charted, in these pages and in his book *The Bus We Loved* – it swiftly won a position of affectionate recognition both at home and abroad that none of its predecessors had managed. Its continued popularity was demonstrated in 2002, when widespread protests greeted the announcement that the Routemaster was to be withdrawn from regular commuter service because of concerns over pollution, congestion and, in particular, accessibility to disabled people.

To many Londoners – including those who, like Ralf Obergfell, were born and raised elsewhere – the notion of the city without the RM was an upsetting one that called for action. In Obergfell's case, this took the form of an effort to capture at least a taste of the pleasures the vehicle had to offer before it disappeared from the capital's streets. The photographs reproduced here are a small fraction of the images he recorded during the final eighteen months of the RM's operation, mostly gathered on the 19 and 38 routes that run between Finsbury Park and Battersea in one case and Hackney and Victoria in the other.

An exercise in neither protest nor nostalgia, the project is a document of the buses' unique and enduring design qualities, and also a record of the RM's interaction with the contemporary London community it served, an interaction whose vividly captured fluidity and variation were dependent on components absent from the Routemaster's successors: the hop-on, hop-off open back and the presence of conductors. As one reader of *Time Out London* magazine suggested, it's like the difference between analogue and digital. For the new vehicles – including the articulated 'bendy buses' originally designed for use on wide European boulevards rather than the often cramped twists and turns of London's roads – it's either on or off, bus stop or not. The RM had the capacity for intermediary states, allowing its passengers flexibility and adaptation to circumstance. The combination of appealing, sometimes quirky design, personalised passenger service and an adaptive relationship with the streets it toured gave the Routemaster a unique sense of character. At times, from certain angles, it could seem a living thing – a vital part of a vibrant ecosystem – as much as a piece of machinery.

These are the angles that Ralf's pictures capture. His images throb with colour, personality and life, even if their primary subject is a mechanical vehicle. *Last Stop* certainly isn't oblivious to the Routemaster's iconic status as a symbol of London: in these pages we are vividly reminded once again that it can easily hold its own whether positioned beneath the braying hoardings of Piccadilly Circus, before the Houses of Parliament or in juxtaposition to the delicate diameters of the London Eye. But unlike all of these, unlike the pillar box or phone box, the RM is gloriously free, prowling the roads like the biggest beast in the jungle, glimpsed rising majestically out of the flow of traffic or even bearing down on a cyclist like a lion closing in on an antelope.

More often, though, it seems like a friend. 'Welcome', reads one of the many signs on which Obergfell focuses – just one of the many ways in which he looks beyond the bus's iconic outline to pick out the myriad small-scale design features that combined into a uniquely satisfying whole. One aspect of this is the lettering laced throughout these images, usually in the stylishly utilitarian sans-serif fonts that are a signature of London Transport. From the confident gold-on-red 'London' marking the side of a vehicle to the elegant functionality of the buses' yellow-on-black frontal route displays, signage takes its turn in the spotlight here, offered up as thoughtful work worthy of attention in its own right rather than a mere means to an end. The stark 'BUS STOP' painted onto the tarmac of a bus lane seems coarse by comparison.

Obergfell's camera lingers lovingly over numerous details that would seldom be noticed at all during an average commuter's journey but were in fact integral to the RM's appeal: our attention is drawn again and again to the preference for curves over corners, natural colours over neons, the distinctive over the banal. On the exterior of the vehicles, bug-eye headlights and a curved radiator grille can't help but recall a smiling face, while a wing-mirror-and-indicator combo forms an intriguing arrangement of shape and colour.

It's the interior of the vehicle, though, that yields a real treasure trove. The warm red of a leather seat glows in the sunlight, while, in a nocturnal shot, a light bulb bulges out of the ceiling like a friendly boil, casting a soft glow across the nicotine-cream paint around it. The convex mirror at the top of the staircase becomes a bulbous porthole, cheekily reflecting the balding head of a man whose face remains unseen, but for the eyebrows that have been raised into the bottom of the frame – another pair of curves. Railings at the top of the stairs take on a seductive, almost organic quality, the hard metal tempered into strange, curvilinear form; a comparably knobbly window latch also becomes a curiosity when brought to our attention. More metal is made affecting when we see a conductor's hands cradle the chunky heft of a ticket machine with familiar ease: the fingers of the left hand splay across its bulk, while those of the right turn its handle. If you didn't know better, you might take it for some kind of exotic musical instrument.

In a handful of night-time shots, by contrast, the RM loses all detail, depicted instead as a collection of streaks of light careering past road signs, fountains, street corners and lamp posts. Such images pay tribute to the striking part the vehicles played in the nocturnal lightshow of the capital's streets – and not, it must be said, to the sometimes excruciatingly lengthy experience of waiting for a long-overdue service. Faster than a speeding bullet? Pull the other one.

But these photographs aren't solely dedicated to the bus as an object. Just as important is the attention they pay to the Routemaster in its natural environment, on the streets of the capital, and the unique part it played in keeping its life flowing. The key attribute here is the open rear platform that allowed passengers to hop on and off in between stops, granting them a sense of ownership – of their journey, of the city – unavailable to users of the replacement services. More than once, Obergfell captures a passenger balanced in their own intermediary state, apparently hovering in mid-air, one foot on, one foot off, as they board or dismount.

Elsewhere, we see a young conductor standing on the platform, facing the camera. Lit by direct sunlight yet gripping the yellow plastic pole – a latterday replacement for the more aesthetically pleasing chrome original, which takes centre-stage in another shot – he is both inside and outside, a part of the vehicle and a part of the street. That pole crops up again and again, a small gesture of distinction between interior and exterior, a symbol of that analogue fluidity of the RM that forms a major feature of these photos. There are shots of conductors standing sentinel at the pole, seen from inside and outside; one is caught exchanging smiles, and perhaps conversation, with the driver of a black cab, that other icon of London's streets. Divided by that pole, they are united in their ease at navigating the city; the cabbie's open window and lolling elbow even give him a mild echo of the inside–outside permeability the conductor enjoys.

The freedom to choose inside or outside for oneself: look at the pair of men running down the street, away from a bus stop and towards the RM that has just left it, backs turned to us and the bendy bus apparently approaching the stop. Impossible to say whether they'll succeed in boarding, but there's something about the way one of them holds a supporting arm to the other's elbow that makes you hope they do.

If there was ergonomic fluidity in the RM's design and environmental fluidity in the open back, the conductors offered a social fluidity – a multitude of potential interactions made possible by their circulation among the passengers in a way quite different from the one-man crews of newer models. (Indeed, with the introduction of automated swipe-in Oyster cards, there is no longer any need for most passengers to have even the most perfunctory exchange with the driver of a London bus.) *Last Stop* showcases the friendlier faces of this interaction – a conductor shares a joke with a passenger, both mouths wide with laughter – rather than the more confrontational encounters that were also a regular part of the working day.

Last Stop also takes us behind the scenes at the bus depot, showing drivers and conductors away from their posts. There are moments of relaxation and humour that add an extra human dimension to the RM theatre: reading on a patch of grass, playing pool, holding up a plate of well-earned grub. But the proprietary stance that many conductors display while on duty is still very much present, especially in Jet's portrait shots of drivers and conductors with the vehicles they command. Workers stand before or beside their buses, arms crossed or held confidently by their sides, or with a hand resting tenderly on the bus's bonnet. There's a sense of pride here, and teamwork – the sort of affectionate mastery Gainsborough might have found between a man and his horse. (One exterior shot shows a driver mounting his cabin like a steed, while in another image parked vehicles stand in a row, like cavalry waiting for the off, or even guardsmen themselves.) One driver is shown crouching in the entrance to her cab, neatly balanced and composed, entirely at home in her environment.

The range of ethnic backgrounds from which the conductors and drivers come is also worth noting: another part of the Routemaster's heritage, after all, was London Transport's active recruitment of West Indians at the time of the RM's introduction. A whole social history of late twentieth-century London is inscribed into the bus's lifespan, and *Last Stop* provides a snapshot of the final chapter. It's impossible to say today what will be most striking to viewers of these images fifty years from now – what they will be able to read into the clothes, the poses, the street scenes whose peculiarities are so commonplace to us now as to be invisible. But these aspects of the Routemaster's working life are every bit as important to these photographs as the fine details of the vehicles' construction – perhaps more so, as we can revisit the machines in their retirement, but not the living nexus of social, environmental and design elements that they constituted while in regular service.

It's tempting now to look back on some of these shots with a sense of sadness, not just at their status as records of a time now past, however recently, but at the passing of the machines themselves too. There's no doubt that many people felt emotional at the passing of the bus: one visitor to the *Last Stop* website described blinking back tears as they perused the images on show. The heroic pose of a green number 19 shot from ground level, for instance, is undercut by the 'Not In Service' sign on its façade. Among the most sobering images are those taken in the garage as the decommissioned Routemasters are dismantled. Elsewhere we have seen the buses being treated while on service – one shot shows an RM with its bonnet open and engine exposed, as if undergoing open-heart surgery – but under these circumstances it feels more like peering into a morgue. Deep gouges score the vehicles' bodywork in ominous compositions of red and black, while rows of un-upholstered seat frames take on a skeletal air. Is it fanciful to see echoes of innards in the parts that spill out, or of a ribcage in the rows of tyres stacked against a graffiti-scrawled panel? And call me morbid, but I can't help seeing a skull in the RM that has lost its radiator grille and windscreens.

But it would be wrong to dwell on such thoughts. First and foremost, *Last Stop* is a celebration of the RM at work, its various aspects captured by Obergfell's eye for the telling detail and his lively sense of space, the alternation between the curious close-up that zeroes in on an item of interest and the bigger frame that locates the vehicle in its natural habitat: the glance exchanged or the ingeniously designed latch versus the moment of flight as a passenger just grabs onto a departing bus. All the small things that add up to a big part of a city that is now a part of its history.

Routemasters can still be seen on London's streets, on tourist-oriented 'heritage routes' with limited reach. No longer, for instance, can an RM be glimpsed sailing across Westminster Bridge. What were once proud masters of the road are now indulged relics, less moving landmarks now than animated museum pieces. Their iconic contours can still be witnessed at first hand, but for an appreciation of the rich, fluid London life that once passed through their open backs, we can turn to the images contained in Ralf Obergfell's *Last Stop*.

Ben Walters wrote about the *Last Stop* website for *Time Out London*, where he was deputy film editor. He has also written books about Orson Welles, *The Office* and *The Big Lebowski*, and regularly contributes to *Sight and Sound*, *Film Quarterly* and other publications.

Right
Anthony James

Ralf Obergfell

I was twelve or thirteen years old when I first spotted the Routemaster, on TV at my parents' house in Staufen, a small town on the edge of the Black Forest in Germany, where I grew up.

I was hit by the striking bright red, the powerful design, with its friendly-looking round curves, the open platform with the chrome pole located in its centre, and the fact that the bus was conductor-operated. To me, the Routemaster conveyed a sense of original London street furniture, a classic piece of art and technology that was loved and valued by Londoners and visitors alike. The Routemaster presented a sense of communal spirit that just made it fun to ride on.

My interest in photography was driven by London and the environment I grew up in. Dad photographed a lot when we were kids, so photography was always around me and my younger brother Marco. Eugen, our father, would teach us some tips and basic elements with regard to exposure and light. We would watch and learn, and eventually started shooting ourselves when he passed his cameras on to us. When he gave me his Minolta X700, I felt a moment of joy, and started taking my first photographs of kids at school and our family surroundings. I used the same camera throughout the *Last Stop* project.

To a few of us Black Forest kids, it was Britain and in particular London that made us feel in awe. From being a teenager, I became attracted to the sound of early '80s English bands like The Cure, Depeche Mode, Duran Duran and Eurythmics. The Punk and New Romantic fashion sense that went with the music seemed outrageous and fun. I decided to move to London to experience and explore my attraction. I had just turned twenty when I arrived in the Big Smoke. The moment I arrived I was hooked on its creative, crazy buzz.

My early London years were spent working in bars. The early '90s were a time of recession: it was hard to find work, especially if you didn't have a good command of the English language. This wasn't German primary school English they spoke here – this was proper London street English. You learned from scratch. After three years, my English seemed good enough for me to start exploring my interest in art and business on an academic level. I studied Advertising and Creative Marketing at the London College of Printing and upon graduation decided to revisit my passion and start working seriously on and with photography.

In 2001, a friend introduced me to Photodebut, a budding London-based art collective that promotes, supports and connects emerging photographers. I submitted some work and in 2002 became one of Photodebut's founding members. Our early meetings were held at the Agency on Charlotte Road in Shoreditch, east London. We would critically analyse one another's work, share ideas and plan projects, exhibitions and educational talks.

At those meetings I became friends with Maxine Beuret and Jet. Max expressed an interest in working on a collaborative project and mentioned that the Routemasters were to be withdrawn from commercial operation. This sent shockwaves through me. We soon realised that the three of us shared a deep-rooted passion for the Routemaster and decided to create a visual record of its last eighteen months.

We began in spring 2004. Shooting both together and individually, we started to accumulate a substantial body of work that captured the interior and exterior design elements of the bus, and the interactions between the passengers and conductors on board. Maxine was forced to conclude her involvement at the end of 2004 as she devoted her efforts to another transport-related project – *The Departure of the Slam Door Train* – but Jet and I continued. Jet concentrated on portraits of drivers and conductors with their vehicles at the depots, while my focus was on the buses' design elements and the unexpected moments that arose during their working days out on the streets.

Above
Depot Parking

The shooting predominantly took place on the Arriva-operated 19 and 38 'brother and sister' routes running between Hackney in the north-east, Victoria in central London and Battersea in the south-west. I loved being on the routes, especially when I became friends with Kathy Mustafa and Phil Geraghty. Kathy worked as a conductor on route 19, Phil on route 38. Some days I'd stay with them from one end of the route to the other and back again. On other days, I'd go jumping on and off, getting onto any Routemaster passing from either direction. It felt like being on a Routemaster rally. The desire to go out there and hunt for those shots felt great.

Once we had produced a comprehensive body of work, we came up with the idea of creating a website. Jet's friend Steven Haycock designed routemasters.co.uk, which was launched in May 2005, though I continued shooting until 9 December 2005, the day regular Routemaster service ended. In April 2006, routemasters.co.uk was permanently archived by the British Library in the name of national heritage.

I was disappointed to learn that Jet didn't want to pursue the idea of a book. She was happy with what we had achieved with the website, but I had always had the idea of publication in the back of my mind. So I decided, with Jet's blessing, to go on alone and try to fulfil my original dream, which had been intensified by the many enquiries routemasters.co.uk received from around the world, asking whether the work was available as a photography book. Jet said if I did manage to create such a book, she would be happy for her images to be used, so I'm pleased that *Last Stop* also includes some of her portrait shots.

Last Stop provided me with great new insights into London. I learned a lot about the role the Routemaster played in the daily lives of the people working and commuting on them. I developed great respect for the people that worked on the buses, witnessing both the joy and abuse they were exposed to every day. I realised that many of the drivers and conductors loved the Routemasters as much as the Londoners and visitors who commuted on them – a love I hoped to re-create with my photographs. I hope you enjoy *Last Stop*.

Left
Five in a Row

Above
Four in a Row

ROUTEMASTER
RM 298

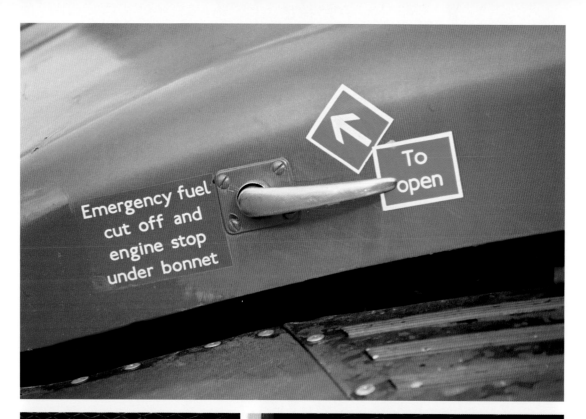

Top left
Nose

Top right
Face

Bottom left
Mouth

Bottom right
Eye

Left
Repair Bay

Right
RM 1145

Above left
Fuel Stop 01

Above right
Fuel Stop 02

This page
Filling Up

Left
Maurice Willmott

Below left
Gillian & Maria

Below
Reading & Standing

46–47   Depot

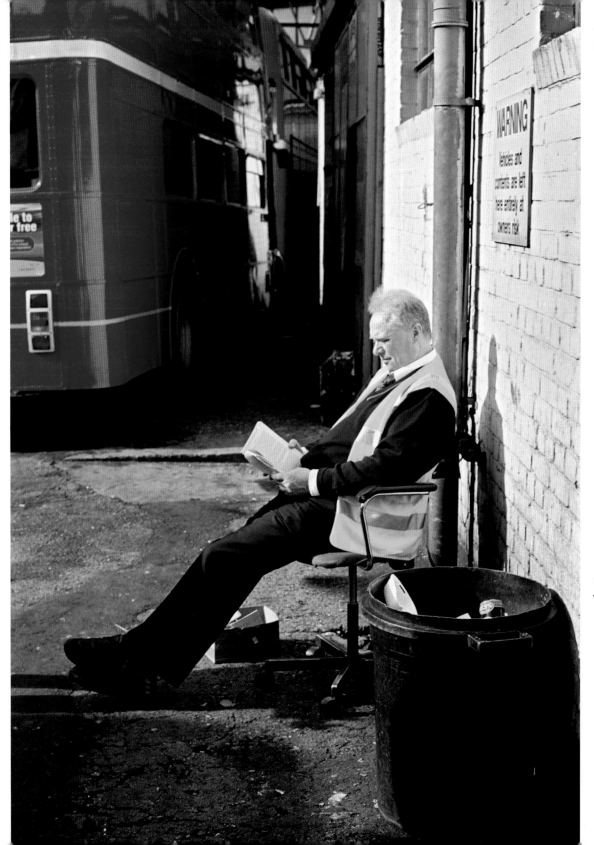

WARNING

Vehicles and
contents are left
here entirely at
owners risk

Next page
Jacques Prince

Left
William N. Kabul

Right
Didier Okou

Left
Steering Wheel

Below
Man Walking By

Right
24 Hour Exit Waiting

Below right
24 Hour Exit Leaving

Left
Hackney Depot

Lenise Musk & Paul E. Geserick

Above
Battersea Kitchen

Right
Battersea Grub

Previous page
K2

Left
Kings Road

Left
Platform Talk

Above
Islington

Right
Happy Cabbie

Left

Hopping off

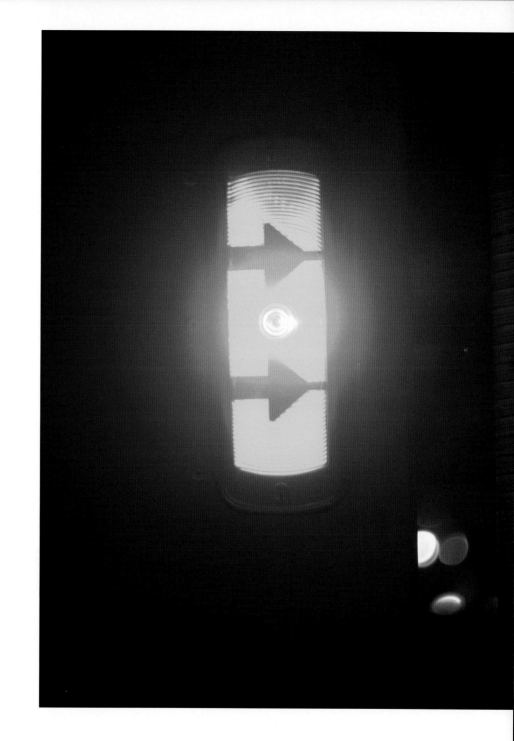

Left
Late Morning

Above
Film Maker

Right
Steam

Previous page
Used Tickets

Right
Summer Afternoon

Left
Widney Ace

Above
Fensterkurbel

Above   Right
Winner for England   Kathy 01

Left
Winter

Left
Bendy Comes

Above
Dry Clean

Right
Ledersitz

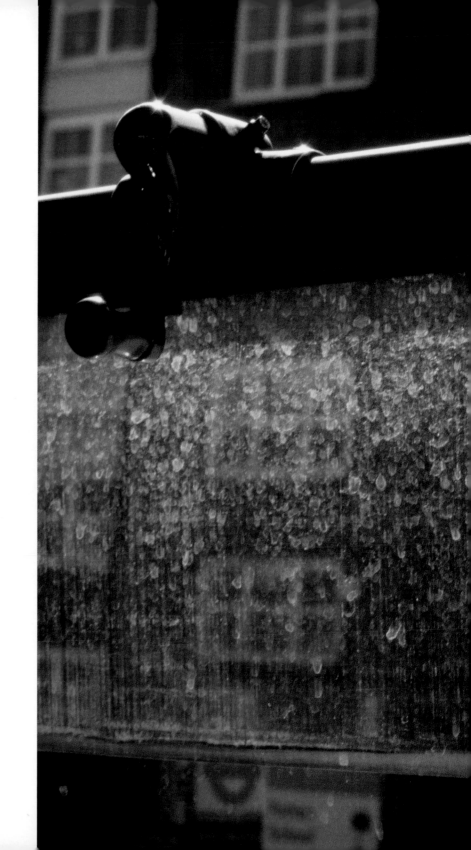

Left
Chrome Lights

Above
Wing 03

Far right
Arrows

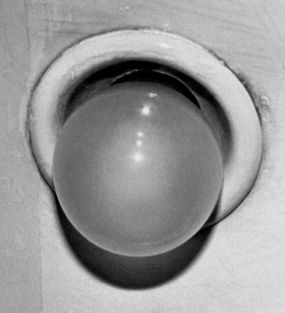

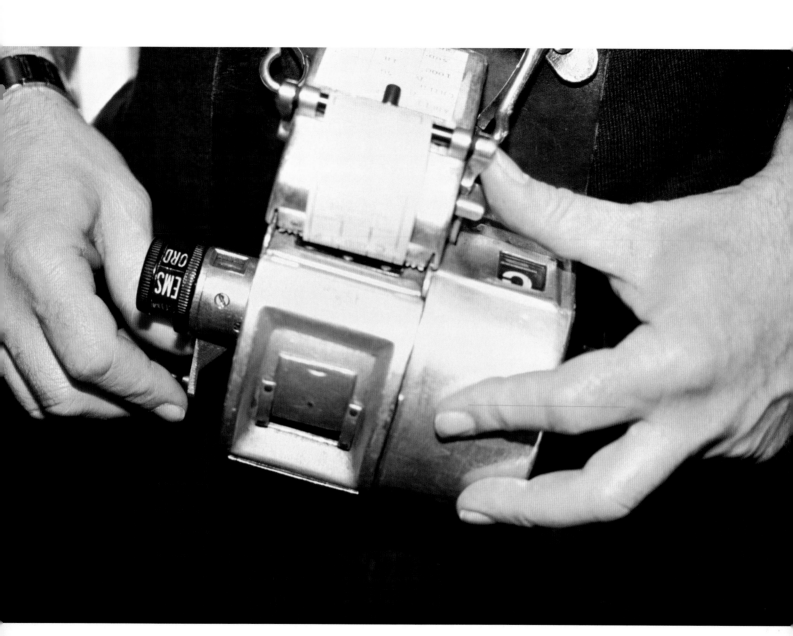

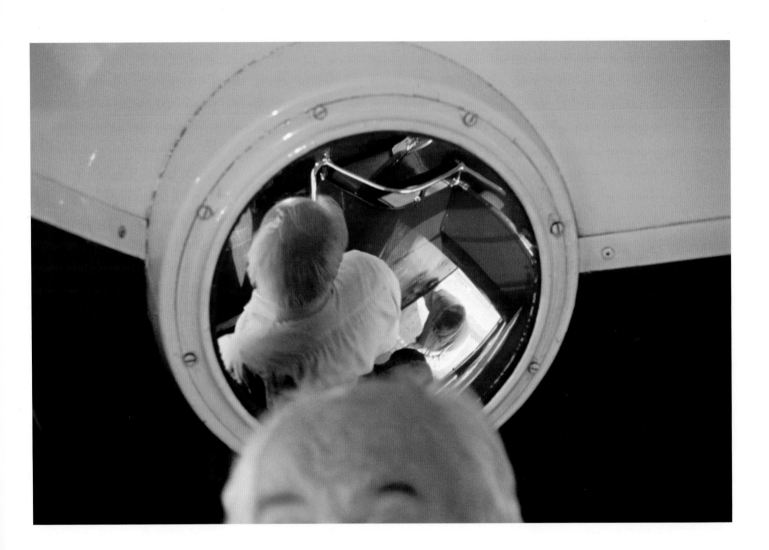

Left
Maxine

Right
Mr Kanabar

Far right
Stairs

Right
Changing Blind

Below
Change

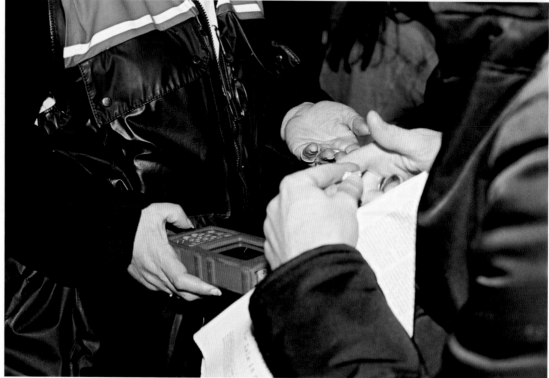

Vivienne Austin

Bell Cord

SALOON
LIGHTING
SWITCHES

Left
Lower Saloon

Previous page
Dead Eye

Left
Mamma Mia

Right
RML 2742

'THE
PERFECT
TICKET FOR
A FEEL-GOOD
NIGHT OUT!'

DAILY TELEGRAPH

www.mamma-mia.com

MAMMA
MIA!

PRINCE OF WALES THEATRE

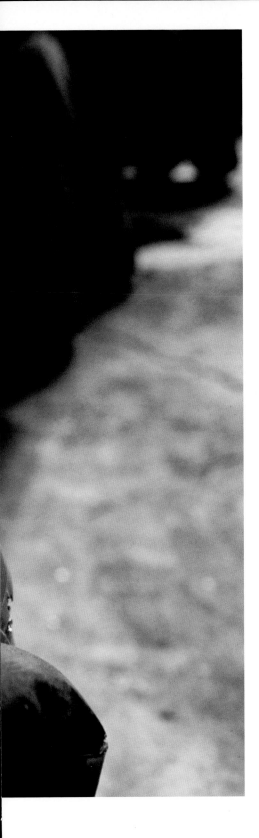

Left
Dead Eye

Left
Driver Cab Skeleton

Above
Assaults

Left
Grille Skeleton

Ralf Obergfell
Born 1971 Freiburg, Germany
Lives and works in London UK.

Solo Exhibition
2008
Last Stop
London Transport Museum, London UK

Group Exhibitions
2006
Stop Moving – Photodebut
Hoxton Square/Brick Lane/
Elephant & Castle, London UK

Petites Morts – Photodebut
Glasshouse Gallery, London UK

2004
Stop Moving – Photodebut
University of the Arts
(London College of Communication)
London UK

2003
Home is where – Photodebut
Four Corners Gallery, London UK

Artist Talk and Presentations
2008
Lecture Programme
(National Diploma Photography)
Art, Design, Media & Performing Arts
Barnet College, London UK

2007
The Individual versus the Collective –
Where do you Stand?
Photodebut in conversation
Photographers' Gallery, London UK

Book
2008
Last Stop

Awards/Honours
2008
Hasselblad Masters Award
Copenhagen, Denmark
Semi Finalist

2007
Paris Photography Award (PX3)
Paris France
Nomination – Emerging Photographer

2005
Grafik Magazine, London UK
Talent Profile (Grafik 129)

British Library, London UK
Last Stop website
www.routemasters.co.uk
Permanently archived in the interest
of national heritage

Works in selected Magazines
Art Review, BBC, Bon, Creative Review,
DayFour, Der Spiegel, Design Week,
Grafik, Herald Tribune, Hotshoe, Midas,
Model Collector, Time Out London,
UNESCO Bangkok, Vogue Korea.

Education
1999
London College of Printing
London Institute, London UK
BA Advertising and Creative Marketing

This catalogue is published in
conjunction with the exhibition
Last Stop, May 2008 – July 2008
London Transport Museum, London UK

My special thanks to:
Per Ljungqvist, my friends and family.

Arriva London, London Transport
Museum, Time Out London.

David Azurdia, Maxine Beuret,
Victoria Brooks, Juan Carlos Cammaert,
Travis Elborough, Jet, Ben Walters.

Art Review (Lupe Fernandez),
Associated Press (Jill Lawless), AXM
(Matt Miles), BBC (Tom Housden),
Ben Brook, British Library (Alison Hill),
CIDA, Creative Review (Mark Sinclair),
Mark Davies, Design Week (Scott
Billings), Deutsche in London, Dewi
Lewis, FT Freiburg, Phil Geraghty,
Grafik (Angharad Lewis), Greenpeace,
Steven Haycock, Hotshoe (Melissa
Dewitt), Doug James, Joe Kerr, Kathy
Mustafa, Zimena Percival, Photodebut,
The Rainforest Foundation, Routemaster
Association, UNESCO, Urban Junkies
(Taryn Ross), Vogue Korea (Sarah Park).

Author photograph by Per Ljungqvist

In memory of Maria Goeppert